E ueen

Dick
Whittington
AND HIS CAT

from Gloucestershire to London

Eileen Fry

THE CHOIR PRESS

First published in the United Kingdom in 2022 by
The Choir Press

ISBN 978-1-78963-321-4

Dick Whittington

This is the story of one of the most influential politicians and leaders in the history of England; and it started in the modest village of Pauntley in Gloucestershire.

Pauntley is a wonderful beginning to our story. A visit there, especially on a sunny day, is a wonderful experience. A turn around in a quiet country lane leads to a step back in time, as the little unpretentious Norman church comes into view. You can pause, take a breath of the pure country air, and (with sheer contentment) feel the nods and prods of the past. Close to the Manor House is Pauntley Church, the place of worship which has so many stories from the past. Inside the stone porch, look carefully and you will see a small cross carved into the entrance. This

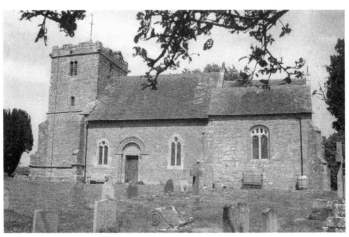

Pauntley Church

Pauntley Church Porch

would be a mark made by the early pilgrims who chose to visit Pauntley as they once walked across Gloucestershire.

In nearby London Road. Gloucester, is a medieval church – St. Mary of Magdalen and, in the porch, there is also has a cross carved, known as medieval graffiti, similar to Pauntley. Now, enter into the church of St. John the Evangelist, Pauntley, and you will be entranced. There is much to absorb. Dick Whittington is definitely identified in the church and there, for all to see, in the west window, is the Fitzwarren Arms belonging to his wife Alice. It is not

London Road Church, Gloucester

really surprising that I once spoke to a lady who claimed her father was adamant that he had once seen the figure of an old farmhand dressed in a smock and breeches, from a time long past, leaving the door of Pauntley Court. The imagination can well play tricks in such a place …

Dick Whittington was the youngest son of three boys born to Sir William Whittington and his wife, Joan. William was the squire of Pauntley, as was his father before him. He had a demanding and challenging life managing the farm and keeping everything, and everyone, in order. It was his life but also a business, and he needed to keep up with the political events of that time.

Year on the Medieval Farm

The first son and heir was named after his father William. As such he would inherit the estate, the land, and the home that went with it.

The second son was Robert. He later became High Sheriff of Gloucester, in the busy town nine miles away.

When Richard was born in 1354, his future was not so obvious; but it would have been expected that somehow he would eventually find a good position worthy of the family name. This he achieved in a magnificent way.

Sadly, Sir William Whittington passed away when Richard, now known as Dick, was only two years old. It would of course, have been a big tragedy for all the family. Joan as a widow and mother needed help to keep the estate in order; William Junior, as eldest son, took over the responsibility of running Pauntley Court; and everyone became even busier. Dick, at such a young age, was left sometimes to his own devices as the rest of the family worked away. Perhaps this is when he began to develop his fondness for animals, and turned to a cat for comfort. We must remember that children then were expected to be seen and not heard.

Now, a mother's loss for a small child is hard indeed, and it is well known what a good friend a cat can be at a time of bereavement. Well, down on the farm at Pauntley, there were many farmyard cats – especially useful to control all the mice and rats.

Throughout time, cats have taken their place in history. For example, The Earl of Caernarfon found the

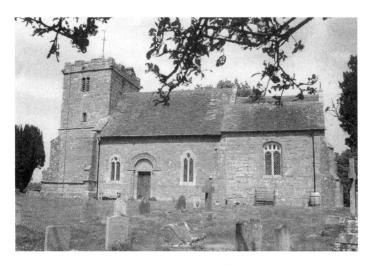

mummified body of a cat as his first discovery, when the tomb of Tutankhamun was revealed. And again, a humble farm cat must have been more than pleased to attach itself to a little boy needing love, comfort, and cuddles!

Romans in Gloucester

The bustling City of Gloucester was as busy a place of commerce in the 14th century, as it had been for many years. The Romans had wisely decided to take over the area and, during their time of occupation, they built a

Romans in Gloucester

place which made them proud. When eventually the Romans left Gloucester, it was a city with a fine strong stone wall encircling the many beautiful buildings. There were statues, and many places of commerce. Roads, squares, and houses were well planned. There was a garrison for the soldiers, and even a mint for making money at Kingsholm, now the home of Rugby in Gloucester. It is claimed that there was even a group of secret Christians who met in a house on the site which now is the Church of St. Mary de Lode. Then, the river ran close by that site. Christianity at that time was illegal and against the state of Rome. Burial places were left behind by the Romans both in and out of the walls. Even today, they are making fresh discoveries of the ancient past under the ever-watchful eye of Andrew Armstrong, the city archaeologist. The Romans also built many roads across England, connecting Gloucester to Cirencester, and then onto London. They also left a great trading network for us to expand.

This business link previously forged by the Romans continued on, and was well used when Whittington was a young man.

It was the accepted choice of the local gentry to have a country estate, and also a town house in the City of Gloucester. Young Dick's older brother, Robert, had such a home in the Westgate area. It was ideally placed near to the magnificent cathedral, and not far from the original centre known as 'The Cross', named after the Cross of Christ. From The Cross there is Northgate, Southgate, Eastgate and Westgate. Travellers would

stop off at busy Gloucester and spend a night or two in one of the city inns. They would meet up with other folk on the way to sell their wares in busy London. Pilgrims, too, would make a journey to visit Gloucester Cathedral. There was a special pilgrims entrance – a doorway and path for them to use – because they were often dirty, smelly, and muddy after their long walk.

Gloucester was quite a place for a week-end break or a pilgrim's holiday. Contacts were made and deals finalised; new friends made and old friends to catch up with; local ale would certainly be in demand. Beer, cider, and mead would have been more in supply and safer than water or milk. It would have been more fun too.

Even the monks in the cathedral even drank small beer. The they also provided the only medical care for the sick, and grew herbs in the abbey gardens to heal illnesses. This was Gloucester at the time Dick left for his big adventure.

The decision is made

Dick spent his childhood in Pauntley, and some of his time with his big brother Robert, in Gloucester, soon becoming a prominent figure in local politics, as well as being given the title and responsibilities of High Sheriff. The Whittington family had contacts with Sir John Fitzwarren who had his roots in Gloucestershire but was now a rich London merchant, trading overseas. Robert knew that his young brother Dick needed to make a move in order to secure his future. Dick was a bright lad, but he needed an opening. It was decided that an apprenticeship within the route taken by Sir John would be a chance not to be missed. Dick was only 13 at the time, so the family knew it would be a tough call. There would be no special favours, the hours would be everlasting, and it would be seven years of long hard graft before making a decent wage. On the other hand, it was an opportunity of a lifetime, and he would have to make the break with his present life.

The journey from Gloucester to London

The wool trade in England was doing very well indeed. Sheep thrived in Gloucestershire and provided the much needed wool used to make fine clothes for fashionable London nobles. Trade overseas was rapidly expanding. London was a busy business centre, full of opportunities.

It was necessary to take the sheep from local areas, and this was the only way to drive them across the countryside. The animals were then in the best

Herding sheep on the way to London

possible condition when they arrived to market. Thus, the 'Drovers Way', as it was known, became well established. A caravan of wool carriers joined up together as a group then made their stop at Gloucester for a break. It was safer to travel in numbers in case they met robbers or thieves on the way. They were ready to put up a fight and defend themselves. There is safety in numbers when making any journey. They went on their way with Northleach becoming another place to rest.

The steady, well organised journey from Gloucester to London took about five days of walking, and the stops along the way were regular and planned, as much as a walking group today would make progress, in fact. The party of sheep, men and young lads too, probably had good fun – especially if the weather was good. Then again, there was safety in numbers; they could support each other. They knew when they handed over the sheep they would be well received, and return home with a heavy purse. Robert would have been happy to send young Dick to London along with the drovers; and would have been pleased to pay for his care on the journey.

Now we ask the question, did he actually take along his cat with him on this trip? It may well have been so;. After all, as far as Dick was concerned, it would have provided the emotional support he needed. He may well have only agreed to go as long as his cat went too. The cat could have walked along next to him or been carried by Dick if weary. It would have been an ideal companion.

London and a new life

Dick arrived in London at only 13 years of age; not an easy job for a lad from the country. He found himself at the beginning of a challenging career. It was considered to be a privilege to be an apprentice in the City of London. Each apprentice had to take an oath of industry, obedience and duty, and the discipline was strict. The hours were from dawn to dusk. Sunday was the only break and, on this day, the young boys were expected to attend a place of worship, and then they could rest.

London City Gate

Dick must have found this new life very hard. However keen he was to impress. He had been told the streets of London were paved with gold, but he did not see much of this as he began to work. No doubt the other boys tormented him at times for his country accent and style of dress. He no longer had his big brother at hand to turn to, and the work was strenuous, the hours long and the food nowhere near as good and plentiful as on the farm in Pauntley. It would have been no surprise if, one day, he decided he would head back home. It is claimed he began to look for a road out of London. He had had enough, so he would return back to Gloucester – if only he could find the right road.

Suddenly, in the distance, he heard a wonderful peal of church bells ringing loud and clear. He stopped and stood still in his tracks, to listen. Church bells would have been a familiar sound wherever he travelled. This time, they seemed to be playing out a message especially for him. The bells were saying "Turn again Whittington, thou worthy citizen, thrice mayor of London". Dick paused and calmed down, angry with himself for his thoughts of giving up. The bells were real to him, so he went back to make a fresh start (no one had noticed his absence). His cat was waiting for him and needed a feed. Dick decided this time there would be no more turning back. His mind was made up, he would give his best effort, and from then on life began to improve.

When he got the chance, either when running errands or on Sundays, Dick would explore the big city. Slowly, he began to recognise the big buildings, and visit the marketplaces. The Port of London was fascinating. He liked to watch the sailors from strange lands, loading and unloading their cargo. It reminded him at times of his old home at Gloucester and the trading there. London of course was much bigger. He sometimes chatted to the sailors: they did not always understand his English tongue, but were pleased to be friendly. He learned a lot from them, and made notes of the different cargos and their destinations.

Dick grew bigger and stronger, he began to love the work. He realised that his employer was a very successful man. Sometimes, Master Fitzwarren would stop and ask Richard about Gloucestershire and how he was getting on. Dick realised he was a kind man, especially when he found him a place to live in his own household and sent him food. Dick was for somewhile living in a garret at the top of his master's house but, of course, this is where his cat proved useful when catching the mice so that he could at least have a good night's sleep.

Success in the city

Dick Whittington soon learnt his trade, and served his seven years under Sir John Fitzwarren. The two men got on very well, and their business knowledge and connections just took off. Sir John included Dick, who became successful in his own right, almost as a member of his own family. It was time to become an independent trader. He took on his own apprentices, and his rise was meteoric. Money, investment, and trading became second nature to the young man from Gloucestershire. Everything he touched did in fact seem to turn to gold. He took advantage of every opportunity. Soon he was selling fine cloths, silks satins, and velvets – all the fine materials that were in big demand from Royal European nobility. English wool, too, was marketed to eager customers; especially on the continent. The quality was second to none.

Trading in London

Richard soon became a very wealthy man, but he did not become careless; it did not go to his head. Soon, the king himself was depending on his generosity. He was even requested to go with the king to Nottingham on a very delicate matter of money mismanagement, involving land belonging to the City of London. He gave his advice, and the matter was resolved. He became what we would now call the king's financial adviser. Dick then was appointed as the Sheriff of London, and also a member of the worshipful company of Mercers. After the sad death of the Mayor of London, named Adam Bamme, in June 1397, Dick Whittington was asked to take his place. Once again, once again the king found himself in big financial trouble, so Dick helped out with a large loan of £10,000 which, at that time, was a fortune indeed. Then he was formally elected mayor for the first time and further loans were made to the king.

The war with France at the battle of Agincourt ended in a victory for England. This was only made possible through the generosity of Dick Whittington. It was noted in history as the King saying to Dick "Never had a Prince such a subject" whereupon the reply came from Dick "Never had a subject such a King". They certainly had a good working relationship and, because of his generous loans, Dick was made exempt from paying taxes on his exports; so his generosity proved beneficial to everyone.

The benefactor

Dick Whittington, because of his total commitment to his many business activities, and his dedication in making London a better place, became an icon in his time. He must have become the most popular man in London. He was always looking out for ways to improve the status of the city. He was also very concerned with the social care of the citizens. He knew he could help by spending his profits in practical ways.

Richard was now living in the parish of St. Michael Paternoster. He was a well-established merchant, politician, and friend of the king. He also found time to marry Alice Fitzwarren, the daughter of his former boss and master. A good marriage would have cemented his status even more. It was a very good move. Everyone knows behind every good man there is the love of a good woman. He was such a man of the people, everywhere he went he saw the poverty and deprivation of the working class.

St Michael Paternoster

He was perhaps inspired probably by the springs of water in the countryside of Gloucestershire when he set about providing water fountains for drinking in the streets of London. The taps in St. Giles, Cripplegate were a real asset. It was also his idea to establish a library of books at Greyfriars, in Cripplegate. What a great idea that was … St. Bartholomew's hospital, originally founded in 1123, had fallen into a sad state of disrepair. So, this too, was rebuilt and used for the common good. Dick Whittington was deeply affected and distressed by the suffering caused to prisoners in the Newgate Prison. The insanitary conditions were appalling, causing many deaths. This was put right at his own expense and supervision.

A new hospital was built especially for unmarried mothers within St. Thomas's Hospital. Dick funded a drainage system, and he also had the foresight to see the need for public toilets. The very first such amenity offered a large public area with seating for no less than

129 people in a large communal space; not really acceptable today, but it must have been an incredible service where previously there had been nothing.

It would do well to remember Dick Whittington next time we have a need for a public convenience, or want to go to a public library. No wonder he was so popular. The king also made him responsible for overseeing the renovations of the magnificent Westminster Abbey. The nave had been open to the sky and in a state of disrepair until Dick gave it his attention, and thus it was restored.

Our hero also arranged for his own church of St. Michaels to provide, next door, a college for a small group of secular priests. All he asked in return was that the order would pray for the souls of Dick Whittington and his wife Alice forever.

Dick was also mindful of the needs of young apprentices. When necessary, he gave accommodation to his apprentices in his own home. He passed a law making it illegal to expect apprentices to wash animal skins in the River Thames in cold or wet weather, because many young boys had died through hypothermia or drowning in the strong river currents – it is hard to believe how hard life could be for boys expected to be men at 13 years of age. The list of his good deeds goes on. There were other acts of kindness, some known, and others forgotten; but we have the record of a good, just, and compassionate man who sincerely worked for the common good, whether it was for king or commoner. He loved all the people and did not hold back on his own time or money.

Apprentice by the River

The King trusted him to oversee every building and restoration work undertaken in his time. His taste and skills were second to none. He understood construction, and every aspect of the building trade. The work with the Mercers in London was paramount. He involved himself with his fellow traders in every way possible. They were a very social group of men, so the meetings and get-togethers must have been constant. Every night was surely a party for Dick Whittington. No doubt he was invited to be guest speaker on a very regular basis. His name was surely on the top of everyone's list. His status, with his great wealth; his fashionable outfits; and his close contacts with royalty and nobles, must have given him what we would now call a 'pop star status'. He was the main man, with … 'a finger in every pie'.

The traders liked nothing better than to show off their products. It was great for publicity, when a colourful and magnificent procession paraded through the city, preceded by a float with a young woman smiling at the crowds, became a yearly event. Londoners clapped, cheered, and partied. This tradition carries on even to this day. The Lord Mayor's Show in our own time is even more of a great occasion;

a *great* showcase; an important day in the Calendar of London – a proud tradition. The most admirable thing, however, about Dick Whittington was that he was always a man of the people, and *for* the people. He showed his kindness, and genuinely cared for everyone. He was more than willing to put his hand in his own pocket to make the world a better place. He invested his time and money to improve all that was around him. That is why he deserves our recognition. A fine example for anyone who has roots in Gloucester, London, England and anywhere in the world, even to this day. He saw the future of export and travel. He worked with any country needing his goods, a great man of his time and a popular role model. He was a man of faith, who respected and supported his church, the king and the most of all … the people.

The death Of Whittington

On his death bed in March 1423, Dick Whittington was surrounded by many people. The room was packed even as he passed away. There were his four executors, many of the beneficiaries of his charities, his physician, relatives, and many others crammed into his bedroom, as he gave his last breath. At his request he was buried next to his wife Alice. Sadly, they had no children to succeed them. The funeral and burial took place in the Church of St. Michael Paternoster Royal which benefited greatly from his generosity. The tomb was elaborate and costly.

The church suffered later damage in the Great Fire of London in September 1666. It was eventually restored by Sir Christopher Wren. There was no trace of a tomb; but, after the Second World War was over in 1945, some four years later, the remains of the church tower revealed the mummified body of a cat.

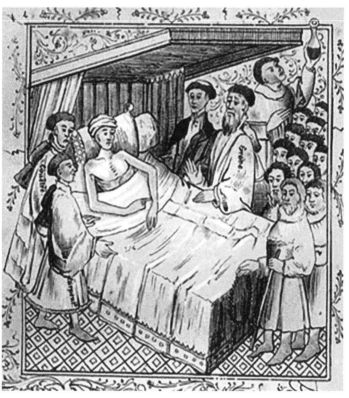

Dick Whittington in his deathbed

Dick Whittington was, in his lifetime, a very meticulous man. And this was never more obvious than when he made his will. He went to great lengths to ensure that as many people would continue to profit from his great wealth. Even to this day, many people even as far away as Gloucestershire are still benefiting from his legacies.

Plays and pantomimes

London in around 1600 was an ever-changing population, growing larger and busier than ever. Music and the theatre were becoming popular, greatly influenced by a young playwright named William Shakespeare no less. His plays were being performed in London, and he was also touring other English

A PLAY IN A LONDON INN YARD, IN THE TIME OF QUEEN ELIZABETH.

From Thornbury's *Old and New London*, Cassell & Co, 1881.

Theatre Scene

towns. Following the trend towards dramatic art, ballads were performed; songs were written and sung. Minstrels were telling stories through their music. Actors and actresses were dressing up and having fun. Travelling groups were always welcome. There was also money to be made.

It was no surprises that song writers and playwrights chose Dick Whittington as a subject for their stories. His memory was still alive. He remained talked about as one of the most popular figures in the history of the city. No doubt parents and grandchildren passed on their own memories of how it was then. What could be a better way to entertain with songs, plays, dancing and singing? Dick Whittington lived on through his exciting rise from a country boy to the richest man in London.

The story of Dick Whittington and his cat began to take place through theatre. The plays were not meant to be a factual history lesson; they were intended to amuse and bring in the crowds, with singing and dancing. There was, however, one constant basis for the entertainment; and that was the title of 'Dick Whittington and his Cat'. The cat lived on throughout the years and never wavered as the main character second only to his master. Now why do you think that was? I believe it was because, of course, there was indeed a cat … The Londoners knew there was a picture in the Mercers Hall dated from 1572, which was recorded at that time but later (sadly) lost, to be replaced by yet another painting at a later date. The first cat painting was of a black and white cat being held by his master. The people who watched the first plays would have already heard about the cat. I am sure the original stories of how Dick came into London would have been given in his own words, as he spoke to the many meetings in the Mercers Hall. He would have been pleased to tell everyone that he had humble beginnings and had walked to London with nothing but his cat. He would have amused his audience and told fellow mercers and apprentices how they, too, could make a good living in the city. From then on, 'Dick Whittington and his Cat' would have become part of the story of London.

There was also at one time a statue of Dick and his Cat engraved into the gate of the notorious Newgate Prison.

Re-living the moment

My own story begins back in Gloucester in 1991. I had just completed a different little book about Dick Whittington and one of my favourite places was the (then) wonderful Folk Museum, full of stories and treasures of our historical city.

I thought a few photographs of Dick Whittington would be useful. Let me explain – not our actual hero, but a young lad of a similar age willing to dress up in a like fashion of that time. I was fortunate in finding just the right lad – my own son, who was actually quite shy, was persuaded he would be perfect for the part. I found an old sheepskin leather jacket together with a leather cap in the bottom of my wardrobe, with which

I had put together an outfit (including a pair of my tights and leather lace up boots). "Spot on," I thought. He certainly looked authentic; but, most of all, he was willing. He, too, was interested in the story and loved the museum.

Simon Pizzey was at that time the official citizen photographer, also having family roots in London. He was extremely good at his job, with plenty of imagination so, he too, was willing to record history. The museum had, at that time, in its collection a wonderful stone carving of Dick Whittington carrying a cat. This exceptional and priceless monument had been found by two workmen in 1862, whilst they were renovating the house opposite the museum. This stonework came from none other than the former house of Dick's elder brother (Robert), the brother who was always there for Dick when he was a young lad and had witnessed his departure to London. He had no doubt been proud to tell everyone in Gloucester about Dick and wanted his image carved within the fireplace, in much the same way as we would now put a family photograph on our mantelpiece.

We entered the Folk Museum, and the stone reminder of the young Dick was brought out to be photographed with my son, David Fry. Simon decided it would be ideal to take the photograph just outside the museum and opposite the place where Dick's brother had once lived. We stood inside the entrance to the museum discussing our plans when, to the amazement of us all, into the museum right on cue stepped the unexpected star of our shoot … a black and white cat. Not only was it a cat; it was a friendly cat that seemed to know how to play the part it had chosen. It went straight up to David just as if it knew the script. Dick picked up the lovely black cat and in an instant Dick Whittington and his cat became a devoted pair ready to walk to London. The moment was recorded by Simon in black and white. It was an unexpected, surreal moment for us all. What a special set of photographs they were, especially as since that time the stone taken from the fireplace which was so unique has disappeared. The valuable piece which had even been sent to London, and then returned to Gloucester for safekeeping, is now gone to goodness knows where.

The cat, we later found out, belonged to a nearby antique shop and was named Christabelle, but had never entered to museum before or since. So, was it a coincidence or something more.? I myself, like the others around at that time will never know, but somehow we were all convinced the cat was prompted to help us out when we needed it most ...

Another animal story

This is another Mayor of Gloucester story involving the same home of Robert Whittington, Dick's brother.

A former city mayor, Roger Langston, had an upholstery business. He needed to find new premises, and where better than the busy Westgate area? He was especially pleased to look over the former mayor's house. Roger said he well remembered the time when he made his first inspection of the premises. He was impressed with the potential. Roger took along with him his little corgi dog named Bonzo, who was always up for a trip, and as soon as he heard his lead rattle he became very excited. He was well trained and would trot along, just happy to be out with his master. That day, Roger recalled, they entered the large ground floor room in the building, and Bonzo immediately began to bark. The barking soon became a howl. He was so disturbed he rushed to the open door and could not be persuaded to go in the room again. Roger laughed and said Bonzo's behaviour was so unusual he did wonder if it was because he encountered Dick Whittington's cat. Who knows?

What next

I do hope you have enjoyed the story of Dick Whittington and will continue to do so, whether it is by careful research or through the laughter and fun of children sitting on the edge of their seats at a Christmas pantomime. Everyone looks at the past with their own eyes. I personally know that I will always feel a hint of nostalgia whenever I visit the Westgate area of Gloucester, and pass by the Folk Museum, or enter the Dick Whittington pub. Gloucester and London will always be connected by the past, present and future.

That cat, too, must always take his rightful place in the history books. Animals of any kind or species have their own thoughts and actions: they exist in their own right, and have a precious part to play in our world. Any person working on a farm or owning a pet will tell you that, like us humans, no two animals are alike. We can feed them or treat them according to their needs, but attachments will always be made.

The unpredicted and frightening pandemic of 2021 in this country taught us the value of an animal as a faithful companion. A dog or a cat for someone living alone became a lifesaver for many. Without words, pets have an intuition often beyond human understanding. They know just the right moment to put up a paw or brush close to you and gaze up with their eyes. It has always been the same, whether they are a named pet or just another member of a flock.

Our hero, Dick, was a man who definitely thought outside the box and went the extra mile for the sake of others. He used his great wealth to benefit the poor and was there for everyone. Kindness, compassion, and love helped him through life when things were tough; and this is what he passed on to others – rich or poor. And, whatever the problem, whether it is our own secret need or even world politics, just like Dick Whittington, it will continue to help us see time through …

So, here's to the memory of Dick and his cat – may they never be separated!

Dick Whittington sitting on a fence.

Dick Whittington statue, Highgate Hill.

The Beginning of Ball games

Dick Whittington as a young lad, pushed out to play in the farmyard, could well have passed his time away kicking around a pig's bladder.

Later, when working as an apprentice in London, he may well have introduced a kick-around, to bond with the lads.

Rugby School in Warwickshire in 1823, first introduced the formalized version of the game, thus giving it a name that would immediately become popular.

Soccer had its first game in 1863, on Barnes Common in London, near to Putney Bridge on the Thames.

Other fun ball games have been played all over England since medieval times. In Bourton on the Water, as an example, men have played a crazy football game, where many of them chase a ball and actually play by kicking around in the river. This is a great tourist attraction, taking place in August. Football, rugby, netball, bowls, golf and table tennis, are just a few of the games played for pleasure, all needing a ball.

Over time, teams, leagues, and competitions have evolved, providing an outlet for all who strive to control a ball to their advantage.

Saturday night has, by tradition, been a time when

game results have been recorded. Football pools began, with fortunes made or lost (depending on luck, and the skills of the players).

Loyalty to the team has become a way of life, and a badge of identity, to players and supporters alike.

Battles have been fought, on and off the pitch, by supporters claiming victory for their own team. Where would we be without it …?

Ball Games Ban in England

Bladders were being kicked around and enjoyed until war reared its ugly head between France and England. In 1415, King Henry V was determined, and his strategy was that the longbow would bring about a successful conclusion. He heard about the young men wasting their spare time kicking around balls made from animal bladders, and decided to put an end to such frivolities. He also banned singing and dancing, declaring that any leisure time should be used for practicing skills with a longbow.

The Yew tree wood was ideal for longbows due to the hard dark wood on the inside of the tree, which was strong and hard, but the light outside skin was soft and pliable. That is why churchyards were obliged to grow as many as possible. Even to this day they still can be seen growing gracefully.

On the 25th October, 1415 (St. Crispin's Day), 6,000 arrows proved their worth, and the battle was won. This period in history was known as "The Hundred Years War".

Time passed by and, once again, ball games, dancing and singing, were enjoyed by the many, just as they are now.

If you ask your grandad about the football he kicked around, he would be pleased to tell you it had a rubber bladder covered by strong dark leather strips on the outside. The inside bladder was blown up by a foot pump. The ball was very hard, strong and dangerous.

Adrian Daglish, Church Restorer and Historian.

Dick Whittington
(The best pantomime story ever)

As our hero Dick left his modest farm life in Pauntley, Gloucestershire, even in his wildest dreams be could never have foreseen how his life story could enthrall and inspire future generations.

As far back as the fifteenth century, strolling players travelled the country, acting out the drama of his rise to fame. The story of how a young man through hard work and a vision for opportunity developed a business importing and exporting goods by means of travelling across the oceans.

He became the richest man in England, even giving money to the King. No wonder this became possibly the best pantomime story ever performed.

A Rugby Requiem

(When the final whistle blows)

The game is finished, no second chance.
Referee has blown the final whistle.
Every hope for a good successful result has reached a conclusion.
Ready or not the match had to end.
There were moments when supporters roared their approval. All was good; you felt great.
The next minute you slipped to offside, the opposition mocked and jeered; you badly needed a conversion before time out.
The pitch had begun with great expectations. The game plan appeared to be perfect. You wanted to badly to be man of the match.
Your clothing and protection were perfectly in place.
Good advice was ringing in your ears. Surely, you're throwing would be second to none.
The end of game was far from easy.
The opposition was often overwhelming – it was an uphill struggle.
Now it is finished. You made the great game your own. Tears were cried when you were sent off. You did your best.
The game of life is over; the crowd are still cheering your effort.
A new season awaits.
Well done. You were a good and faithful servant. You always had your eye on the main chance.
Your great try is history. You will always be a legend.

Medieval Ball Games

Kicking a ball around or throwing it in the air for many, many generations. Football, rugby, netball, table tennis, etc. have evolved into team games, leagues and competitions for many who strive to control a ball to their advantage. Many fortunes have been made or lost depending on the result of the games played. Saturday night was when dad filled in the results of the football pools after cheering his favourite team. Battles had been fought on and off the pitch, by fans claiming their own team's victory.

Playing around in an ancient farmyard, young lads soon found pleasure in kicking, throwing, or punching around a blown up pig's bladder.

Dick Whittington, as a young lad enjoying the outdoor farm life, could well have passed time kicking around a pig's bladder. Later, when working as an apprentice in London, he could well have introduced some sort of a kick around to bond with the lads.

In 1823, Rugby School in Warwickshire first introduced the formalised version of the game of rugby.

And in 1863, Football had its first game on Barnes Common, which near Putney in SE London, near Putney.

There are a lot of fun games that have become a tradition ...

Did it Happen?

When I think about Dick Whittington and his life on the farm (then in Gloucestershire), followed by his meteoric rise to lead so many people, including the king, in London! I wonder … Is it possible that Dick was in any way connected to our wonderful game of rugby? It certainly a highly likely. Dick did, after all, spend his first years as a small boy, living and working on the farm in Pauntley. This was at a time when small children were pushed outside to play and find their own amusements. It is recorded that boys would use a blown-up pig's bladder to throw around, one to another in fun. This game has been going on in a place called Westbourne for at least five hundred years.

When our hero arrived in London, and began his life as a young apprentice, he would have made new friends. This country boy could well have introduced his fellow apprentices to the new game of passing, kicking, and throwing a bladder about. This would have been a fun thing to do after a visit to church on Sundays – the only time off for young lads working in the city. In 1845, Rugby School initiated the first game of Rugby, and created rules of play. But simply kicking and throwing a ball about has certainly been going on since Dick Whittington was a lad.

It was not officially attributed to our hero, but I like to think that this talented young man would have made a great rugby player – yet another talent to make Gloucester City proud to remember this great man. What a thought!

Dick Whittington and His Cat

Finally, a friend recently told me that, as a child in 1960's, she visited relatives in Cannon Street, London. They worked at an ancient establishment of wine merchants (or Vintners) on the banks of the River Thames. As part of the agreement for the wine sellers leasehold of the building, they always had to keep a cat. The oral tradition there, was that Dick Whittington was associated with the place.

Over the years they supplied their goods to lawyers at the Inns of Court and important businessmen. In close proximity are the Vintner's Hall and the Mercer's Guild. The trustees of these guilds worked co-operatively.

Dick Whittington left all his money in trust to the welfare of the poor and elderly, and to Alms-houses supported by grants. These trusts are still running today. He amassed great wealth in his lifetime (over a million pounds, a great deal in today's money) and was able to lend money to three kings (Henry IV, Henry V and Richard II).

When Dick reached Lechlade-on-Thames, in Gloucestershire (on foot), it's plausible that he jumped on to a river boat or barge along with sheep, cattle or goods, to continue his journey to London. River travel was easier than travelling over land. Could he have alighted at this area?

Lightning Source UK Ltd.
Milton Keynes UK
UKHW050921190822
407499UK00006B/245

9 781789 633214